Dedicated to Calee and Micah Joel.
I love you with all of my heart.

Parents, grandparents, guardians;
thank you for taking a few minutes to
teach your child about the Holy Spirit.
I believe that you are planting
seeds that will change the world.

Hi, Holy Spirit! It's a brand new day!
I'm so glad You live in me and tell me what to say.

Your power dwells within me, You teach me wrong from
right. I pray You guide me through this day and I
never leave your sight.

2

I felt a little scared to go to school today,
but You reminded me that because of You I'm brave!

3

This morning we had recess and my friend fell off the swing. He hurt his leg, but You spoke and said the healer lives in me!

I placed my hand upon him and asked for You to help.
Before I knew it, he stood up, and my
friend was feeling well!

My classmates saw what happened, and they all cheered for me. I got to tell them that it was You, Holy Spirit healed his knee!

After that, we went to class and sat down in our seats.
A girl stood up, looked my way, and
said something really mean.

It hurt my feelings really badly and I didn't know
what to say. So I talked to You and
Holy Spirit, you took my sad away!

The school bell rang, so I grabbed my bag and
headed for the bus. I said to Holy Spirit,
"What do You have next for us?"

When I got home, I ran inside to find
something fun to do.

Then my mom came to me
and told me to clean my room!

I was mad at first. I didn't want to clean,
I would rather play outside! Then Holy Spirit
said it's good to obey, so I did what is right.

Hi, Holy Spirit! I enjoyed my day with You.
You taught me lots of things and
You helped me a lot too.

13

Goodnight Holy Spirit, I'll see You when I wake.
You'll walk with me tomorrow,
just like You did today.

14

About the Author

John L'hommedieu is a
youth pastor who resides
in Hurley, Mississippi
with his wife Calee,
and their son, Micah.
His heart is to see people of
all ages walk out the fullness
of their God-given destiny,
and to make Jesus famous.